PIANO FUN
CHRISTMAS HITS
FOR ADULT BEGINNERS

To access audio visit:
www.halleonard.com/mylibrary
Enter Code
5446-6466-6557-2754

ISBN 978-1-4803-5079-3

7777 W. BLUEMOUND RD. P.O. BOX 13819 MILWAUKEE, WI 53213

Visit Hal Leonard Online at
www.halleonard.com

PERFORMANCE NOTES

Introduction

Welcome to *Piano Fun: Christmas Hits for Adult Beginners*, a collection of lead sheets and arrangements for the beginning pianist who has learned how to read music and wants to play easy arrangements of familiar melodies. The left hand accompanying styles include block chords, broken chords and notes that pass between the chords.

About the Orchestrations

There are two orchestrated accompaniment tracks for every song title. The first track is in a slower tempo for the lead sheet, and the second track is slightly faster for the song arrangement. The lead sheet track includes the melody and the arrangement track omits the melody, featuring only orchestrated harmonies.

To access the accompanying audio files, simply go to **www.halleonard.com/mylibrary** and enter the code found on page 1 of this book. This will grant you instant access to every file. You can download to your computer, tablet, or phone, or stream the audio live—and if your device has Flash, you can also use our ***PLAYBACK+*** multi-functional audio player to slow down or speed up the tempo, change keys, or set loop points. This feature is available exclusively from Hal Leonard and is included with the price of this book!

Triads/Chords

- Triads are three note chords and seventh chords have four notes.
- Major triads built on the white piano keys can be divided into three sets:

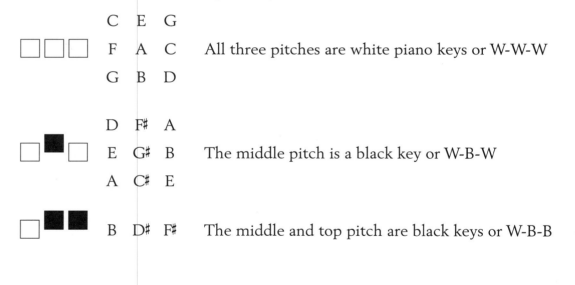

C	E	G
F	A	C	All three pitches are white piano keys or W-W-W
G	B	D

D	F♯	A
E	G♯	B	The middle pitch is a black key or W-B-W
A	C♯	E

B	D♯	F♯	The middle and top pitch are black keys or W-B-B

- Minor triads have a small *m* by the alphabet letter (Cm). They are found by lowering the middle pitch of a major triad.

Cm

- Diminished triads have a small circle by the alphabet letter (C°). They are found by lowering the middle and top pitches of a major triad.

Cdim

- Augmented triads have a small plus by the alphabet letter (C+). They are found by raising the top pitch of a major triad.

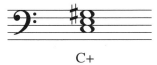

C+

- Seventh chords are spelled with four notes. The bottom note is the root, the next note above is the 3rd, the note above the third is the 5th, and the top note is the 7th.

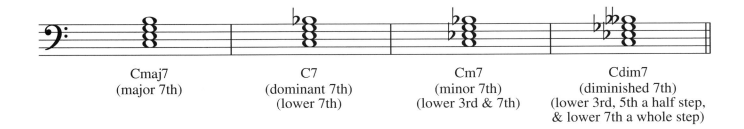

Cmaj7	C7	Cm7	Cdim7
(major 7th)	(dominant 7th)	(minor 7th)	(diminished 7th)
	(lower 7th)	(lower 3rd & 7th)	(lower 3rd, 5th a half step, & lower 7th a whole step)

Repetition and Codas

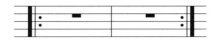

Repeat signs
Play the section more than once. If there is no left repeat sign,
go back to the beginning or to the nearest double bar.

First and second endings
After playing the first ending, repeat the designated section
and jump to the second ending

D.S. al Coda

Dal segno al Coda

Repeat from the 𝄋 sign to the coda sign ⊕.

LEAD SHEETS

Blue Christmas

Words and Music by Billy Hayes
and Jay Johnson

Christmas Time Is Here

from A CHARLIE BROWN CHRISTMAS

Words by Lee Mendelson
Music by Vince Guaraldi

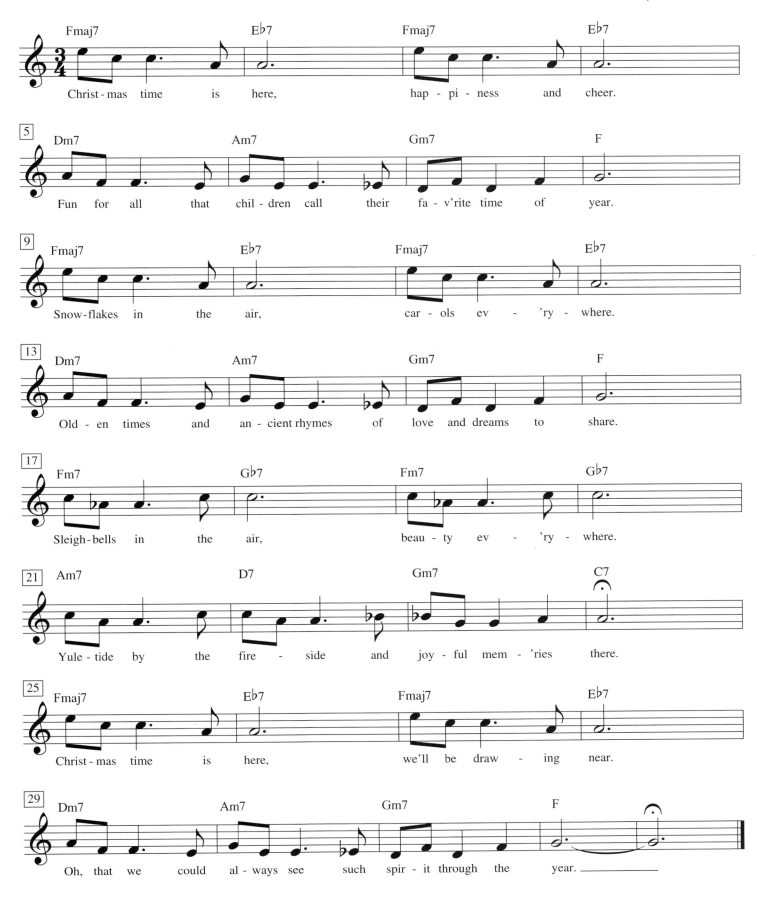

The Christmas Song
(Chestnuts Roasting on an Open Fire)

Music and Lyric by Mel Tormé
and Robert Wells

San - tas's on his way; he's load - ed lots of toys and good - ies on his

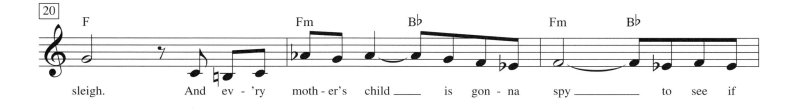

sleigh. And ev - 'ry moth - er's child ____ is gon - na spy ____ to see if

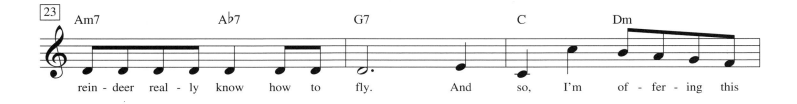

rein - deer real - ly know how to fly. And so, I'm of - fer - ing this

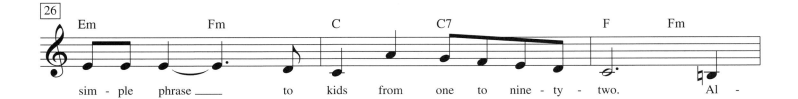

sim - ple phrase ____ to kids from one to nine - ty - two. Al -

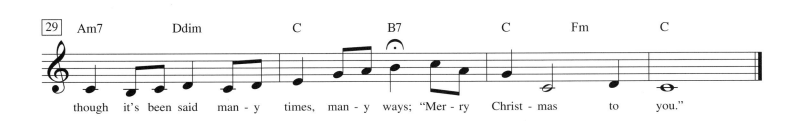

though it's been said man - y times, man - y ways; "Mer - ry Christ - mas to you."

Have Yourself a Merry Little Christmas

Words and Music by Hugh Martin
and Ralph Blane

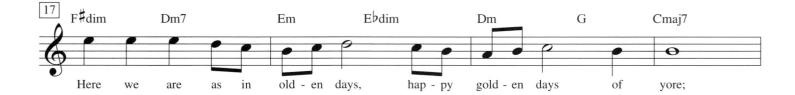

Here we are as in old-en days, hap-py gold-en days of yore;

faith-ful friends who are dear to us gath-er near to us once more.

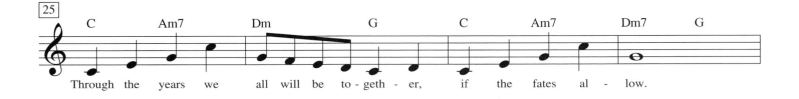

Through the years we all will be to-geth-er, if the fates al-low.

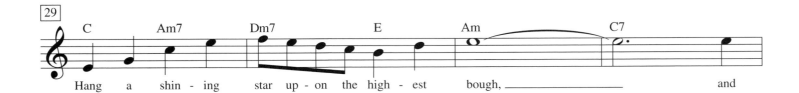

Hang a shin-ing star up-on the high-est bough, _____ and

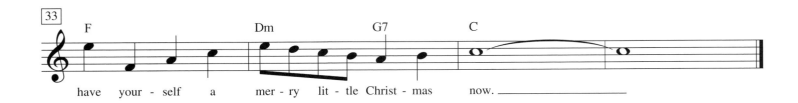

have your-self a mer-ry lit-tle Christ-mas now. _____

Do You Hear What I Hear

Words and Music by Noel Regney
and Gloria Shayne

(There's No Place Like)
Home for the Holidays

Words and Music by Al Stillman
and Robert Allen

I'll Be Home for Christmas

Words and Music by Kim Gannon
and Walter Kent

I Wonder as I Wander

By John Jacob Niles

Jingle Bell Rock

Words and Music by Joe Beal
and Jim Boothe

Silent Night

Words by Joseph Mohr
Translated by John F. Young
Music by Franz X. Gruber

Mary, Did You Know?

Words and Music by Mark Lowry
and Buddy Greene

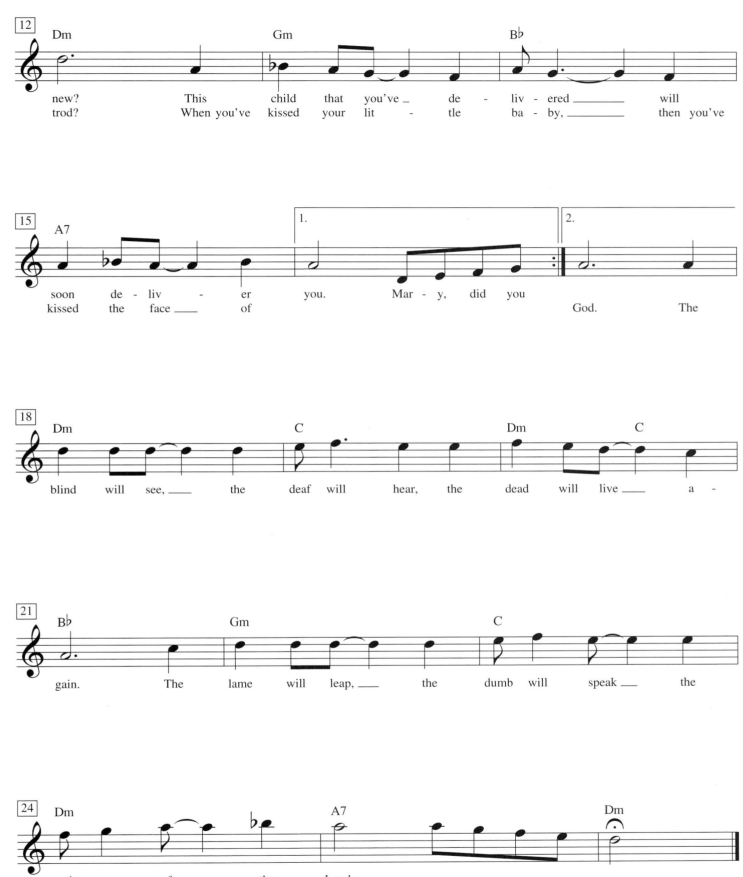

Jingle Jolly Jazz Medley

(Jingle Bells and Jolly Old St. Nicholas)

Arranged by Brenda Dillon

JINGLE BELLS
Words and Music by J. Pierpont

JOLLY OLD ST. NICHOLAS
Traditional 19th Century American Carol

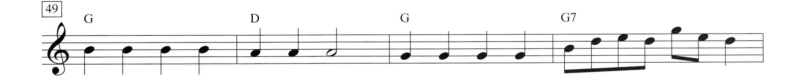

rit.

ARRANGEMENTS

Blue Christmas

Words and Music by Billy Hayes
and Jay Johnson
Arranged by Brenda Dillon

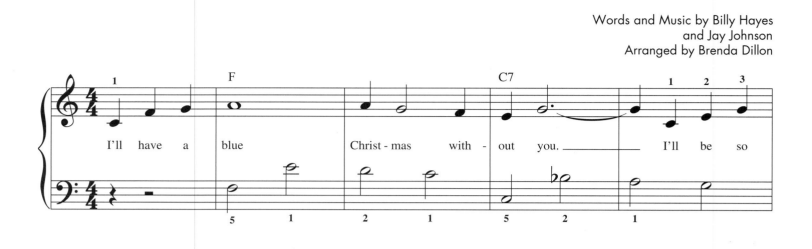

I'll have a blue Christ-mas with-out you. _____ I'll be so

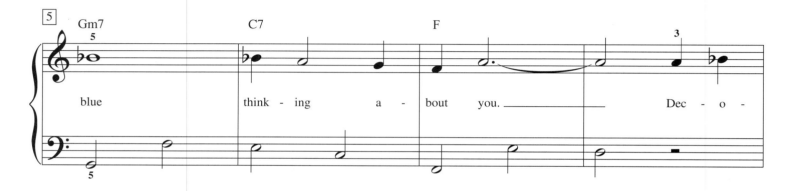

blue think-ing a-bout you. _____ Dec-o-

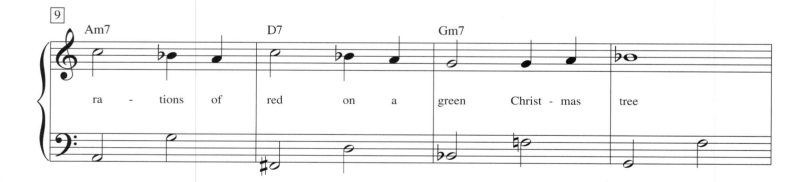

ra - tions of red on a green Christ-mas tree

won't mean a thing if you're not here with me. I'll have a

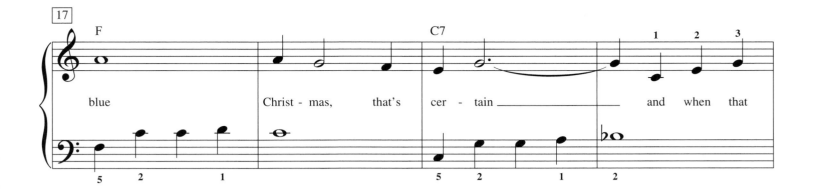

blue   Christ - mas,   that's   cer - tain _____ and   when   that

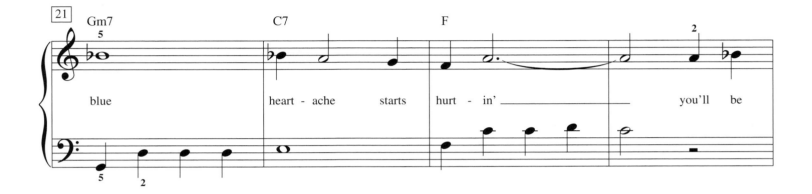

blue   heart - ache   starts   hurt - in' _____ you'll   be

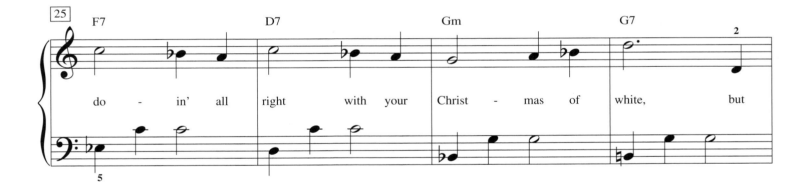

do -   in'   all   right   with   your   Christ -   mas   of   white,   but

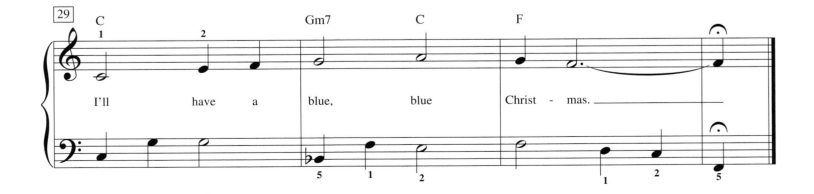

I'll   have   a   blue,   blue   Christ - mas. _____

The Christmas Song

(Chestnuts Roasting on an Open Fire)

Music and Lyric by Mel Tormé
and Robert Wells
Arranged by Brenda Dillon

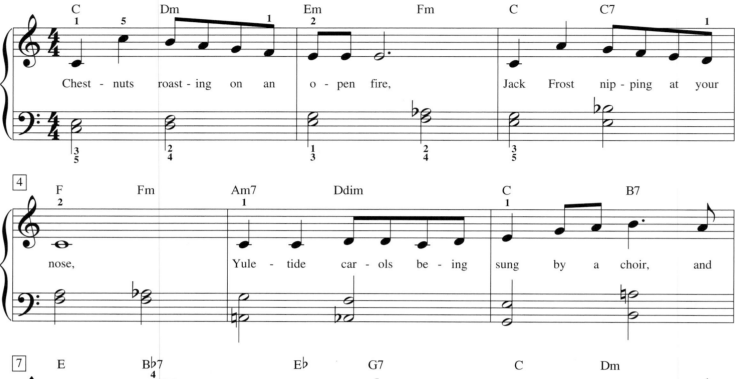

Chest - nuts roast - ing on an o - pen fire, Jack Frost nip - ping at your

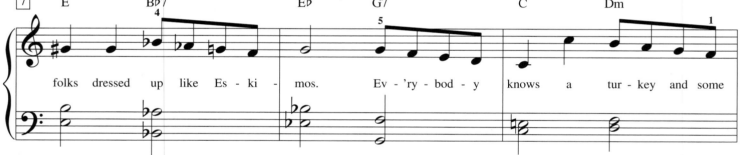

nose, Yule - tide car - ols be - ing sung by a choir, and

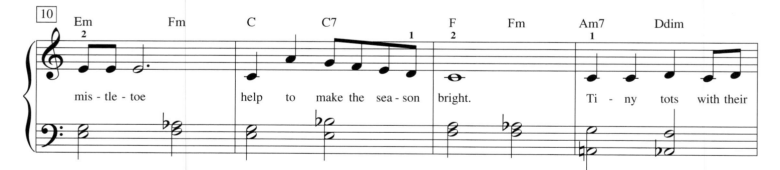

folks dressed up like Es - ki - mos. Ev - 'ry - bod - y knows a tur - key and some

mis - tle - toe help to make the sea - son bright. Ti - ny tots with their

eyes all a - glow will find it hard to sleep to - night. They know that

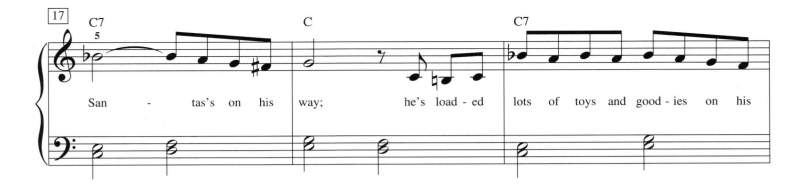

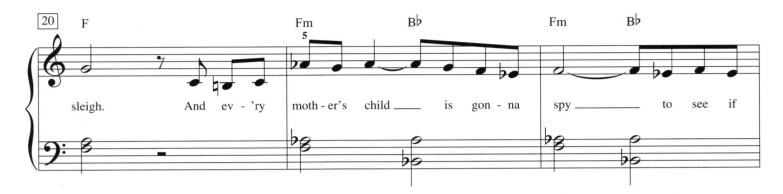

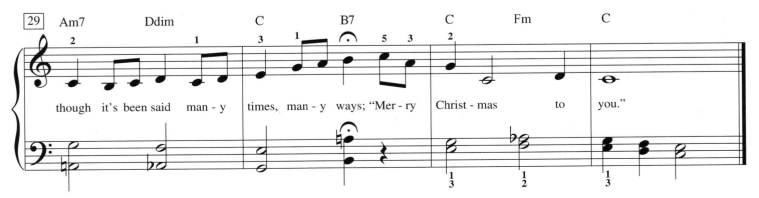

Christmas Time Is Here

from A CHARLIE BROWN CHRISTMAS

Words by Lee Mendelson
Music by Vince Guaraldi
Arranged by Brenda Dillon

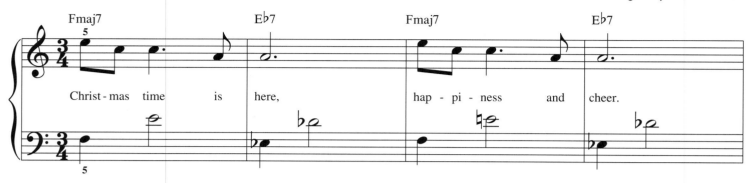

Christ-mas time is here, hap-pi-ness and cheer.

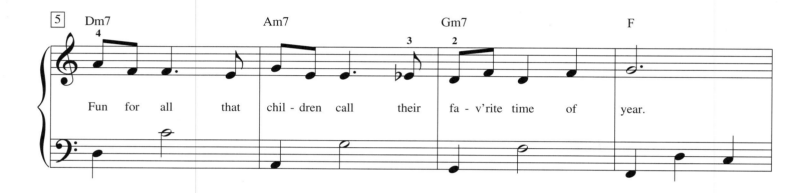

Fun for all that chil-dren call their fa-v'rite time of year.

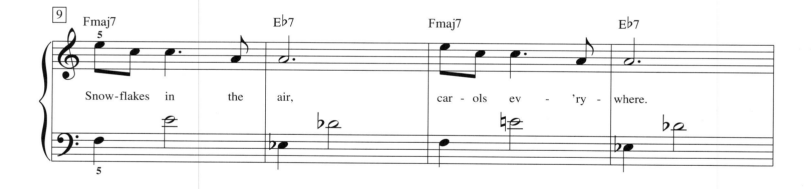

Snow-flakes in the air, car-ols ev-'ry-where.

Old-en times and an-cient rhymes of love and dreams to share.

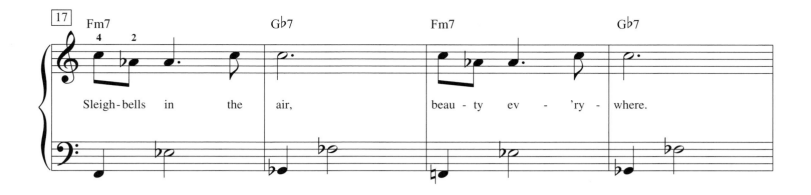

Sleigh-bells in the air, beau-ty ev-'ry-where.

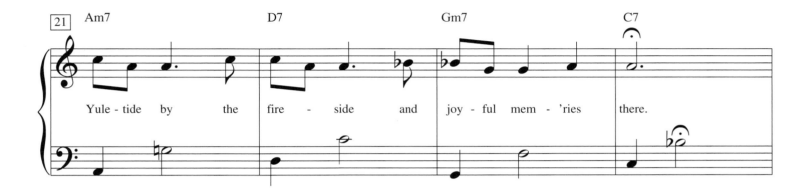

Yule-tide by the fire-side and joy-ful mem-'ries there.

Christ-mas time is here, we'll be draw-ing near.

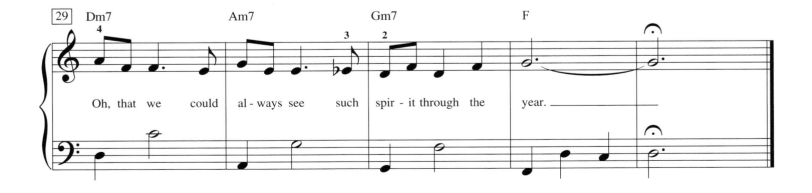

Oh, that we could al-ways see such spir-it through the year.

Do You Hear What I Hear

Words and Music by Noel Regney
and Gloria Shayne
Arranged by Brenda Dillon

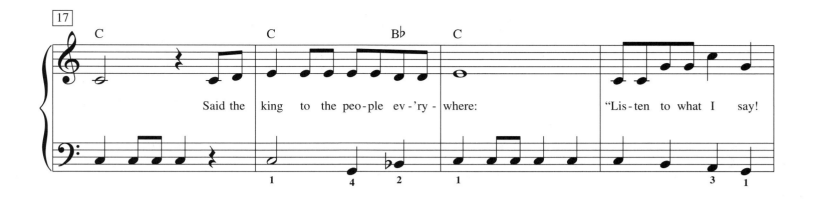

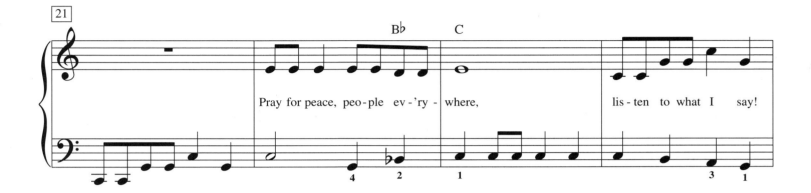

Have Yourself a Merry Little Christmas

Words and Music by Hugh Martin
and Ralph Blane
Arranged by Brenda Dillon

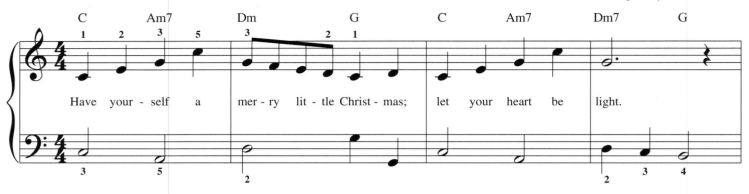

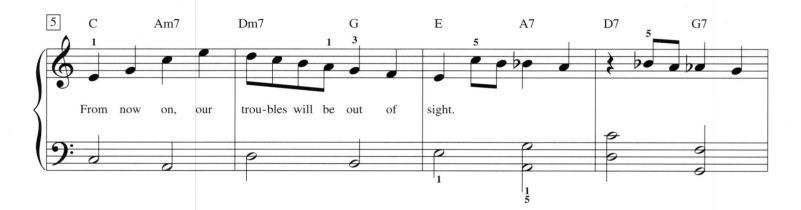

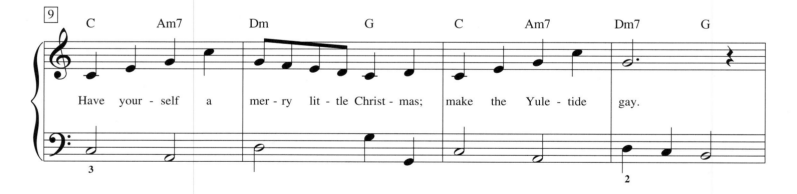

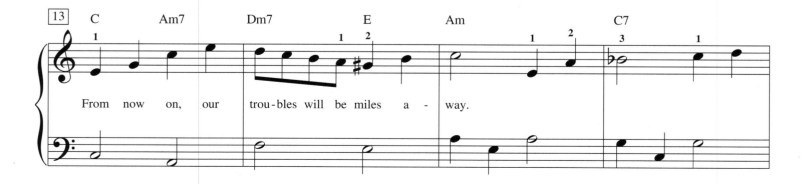

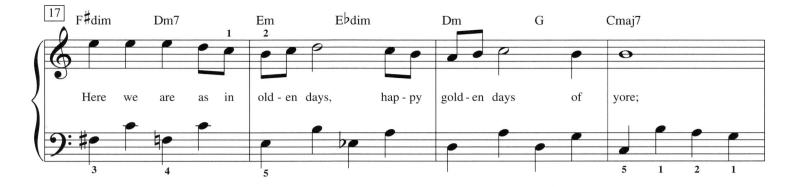

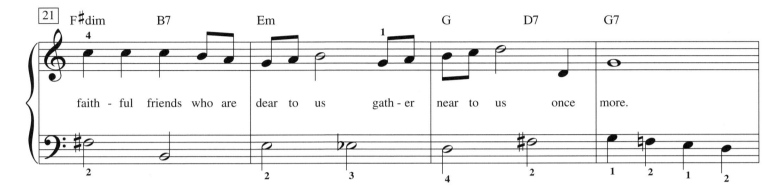

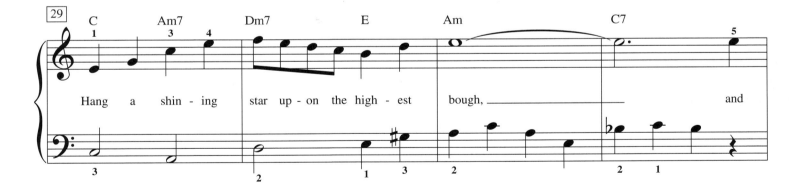

(There's No Place Like)
Home for the Holidays

Words and Music by Al Stillman
and Robert Allen
Arranged by Brenda Dillon

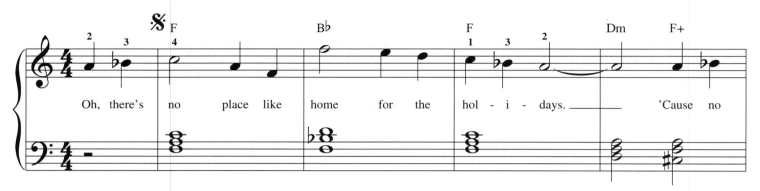

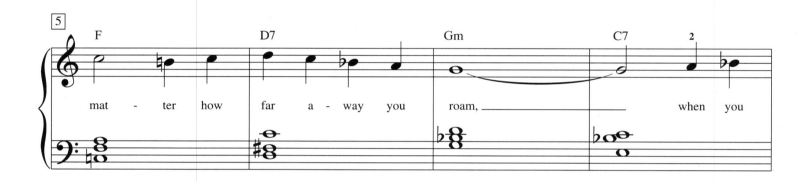

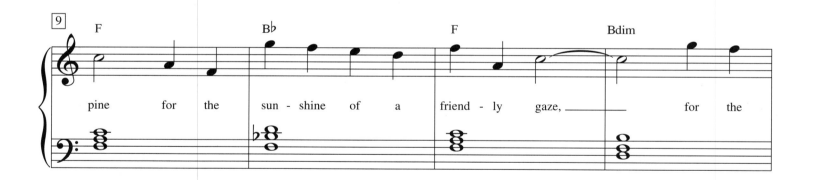

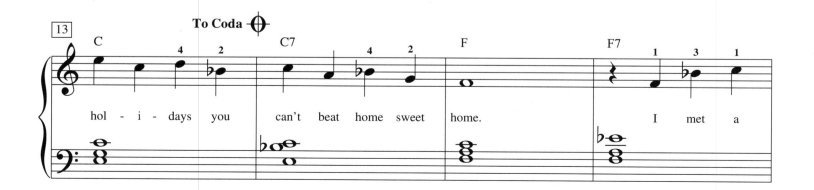

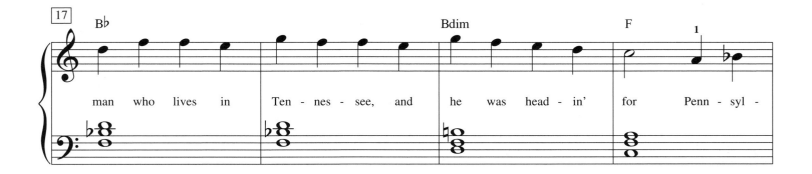

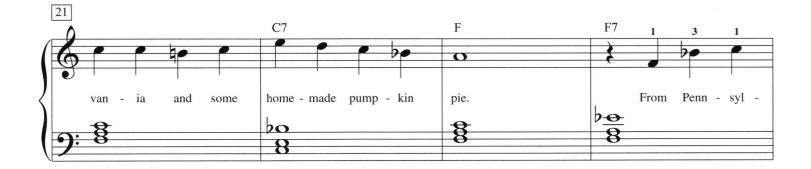

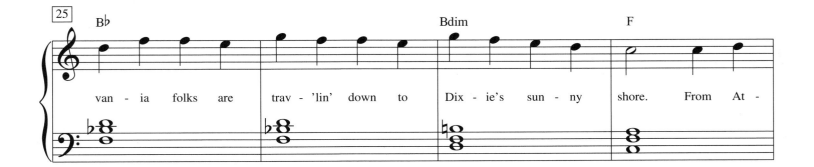

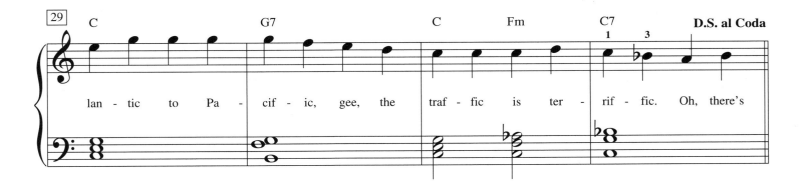

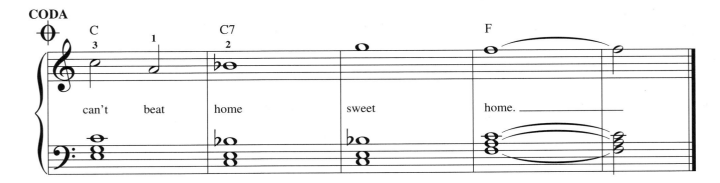

I'll Be Home for Christmas

Words and Music by Kim Gannon
and Walter Kent
Arranged by Brenda Dillon

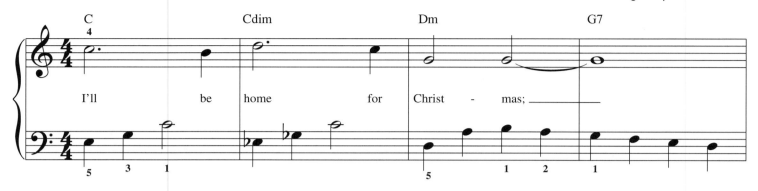

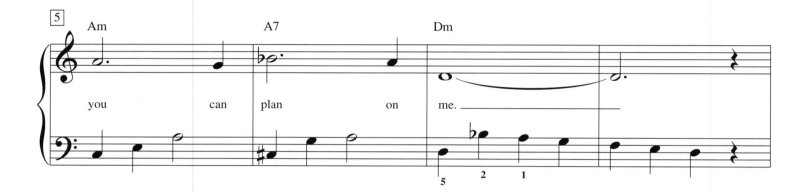

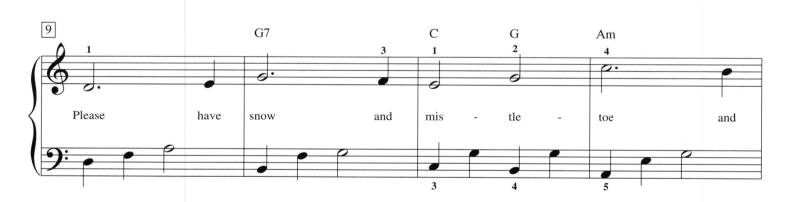

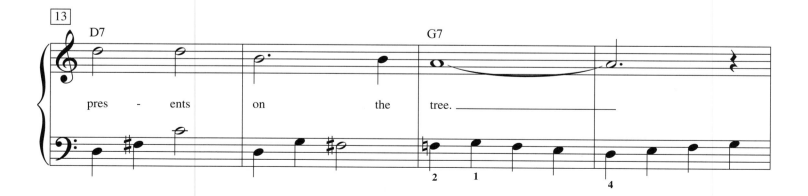

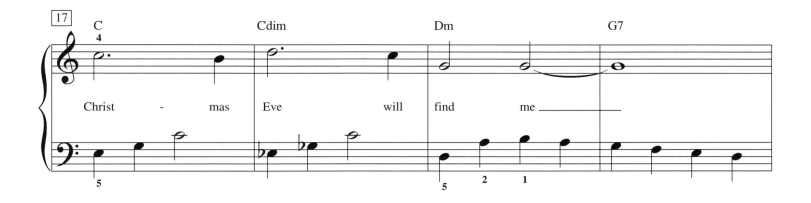

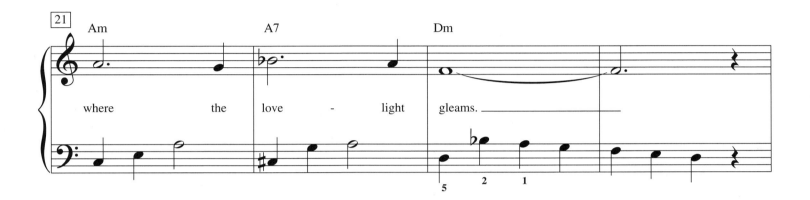

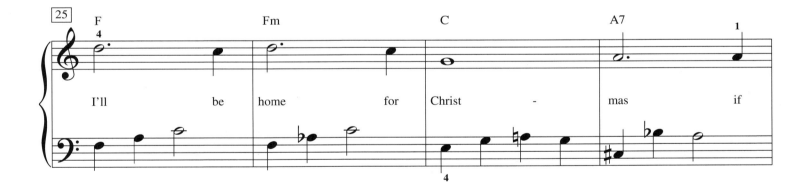

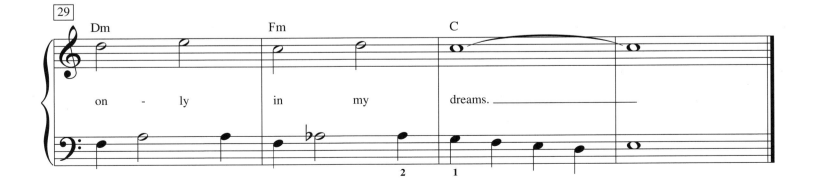

I Wonder as I Wander

By John Jacob Niles
Arranged by Brenda Dillon

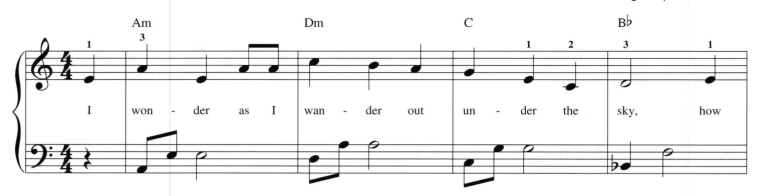

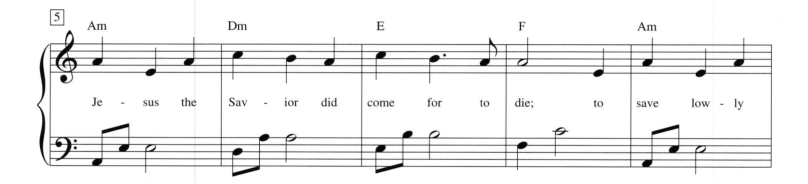

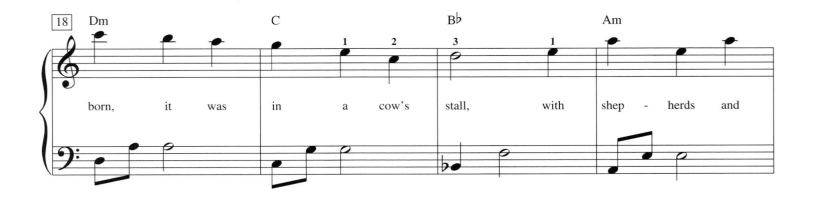

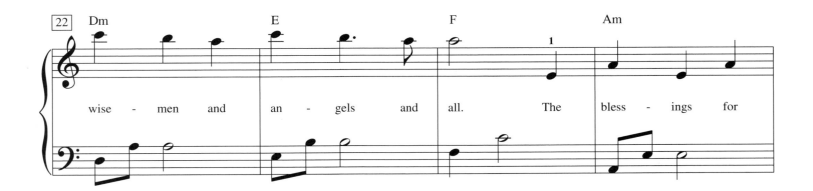

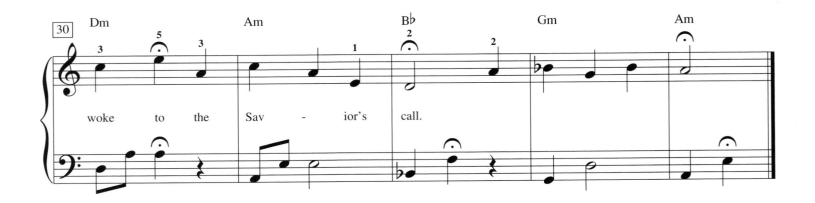

Jingle Bell Rock

Words and Music by Joe Beal
and Jim Boothe
Arranged by Brenda Dillon

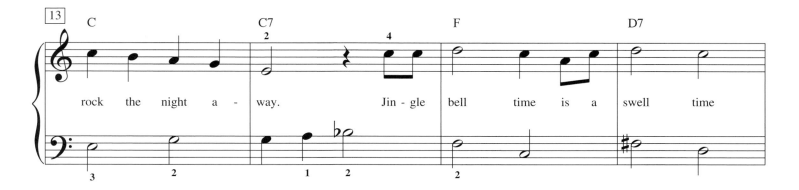

rock the night a - way.   Jin - gle bell time is a swell time

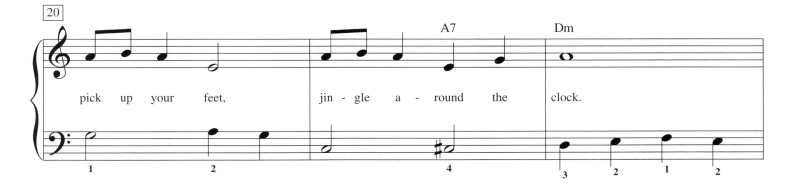

to go glid - in' in a   one - horse sleigh.   Gid - dy - ap, jin - gle horse,

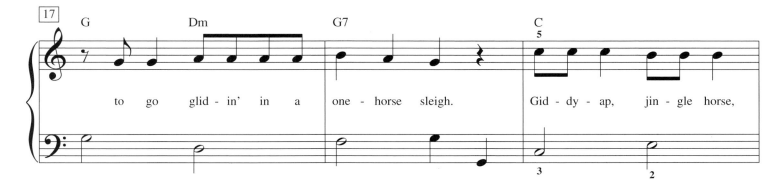

pick up your feet,   jin - gle a - round the   clock.

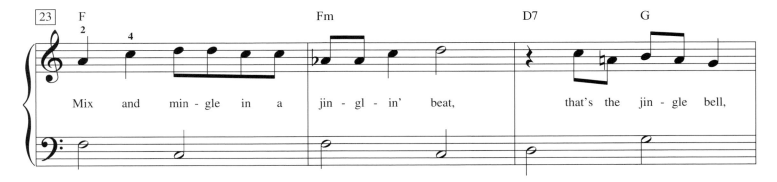

Mix and min - gle in a   jin - gl - in' beat,   that's the jin - gle bell,

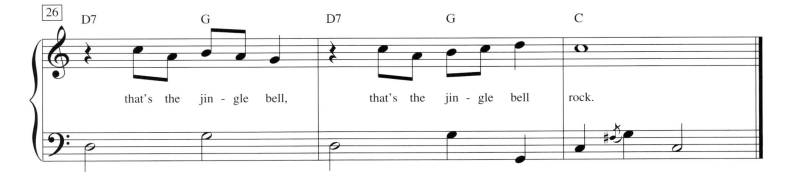

that's the jin - gle bell,   that's the jin - gle bell   rock.

Mary, Did You Know?

Words and Music by Mark Lowry
and Buddy Greene
Arranged by Brenda Dillon

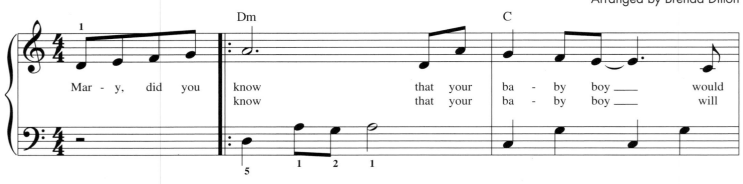

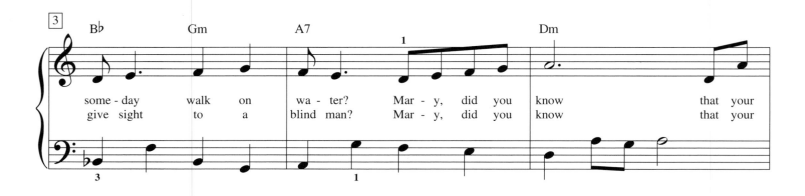

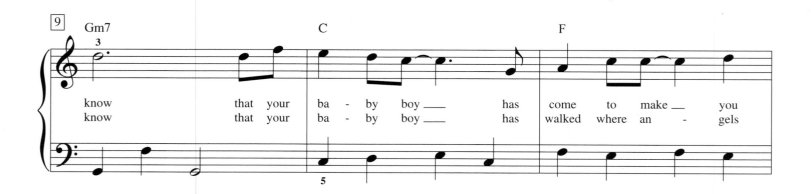

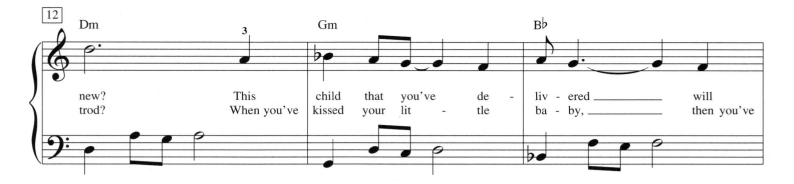

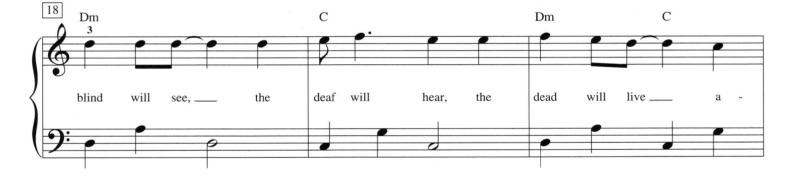

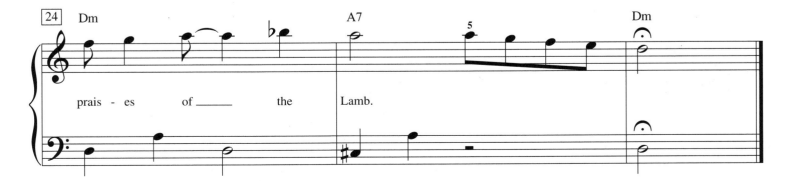

Silent Night

Words by Joseph Mohr
Translated by John F. Young
Music by Franz X. Gruber
Arranged by Brenda Dillon

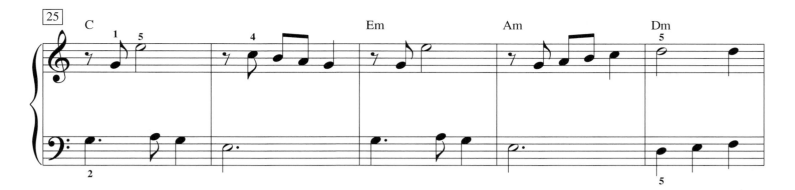

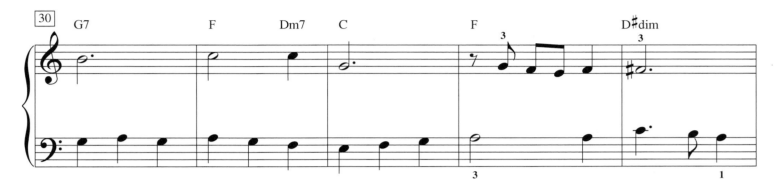

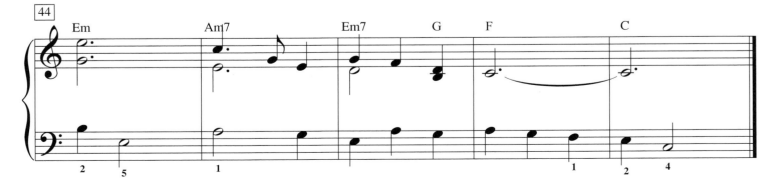

Jingle Jolly Jazz Medley

(Jingle Bells and Jolly Old St. Nicholas)

JINGLE BELLS
Words and Music by J. Pierpont

Arranged by Brenda Dillon

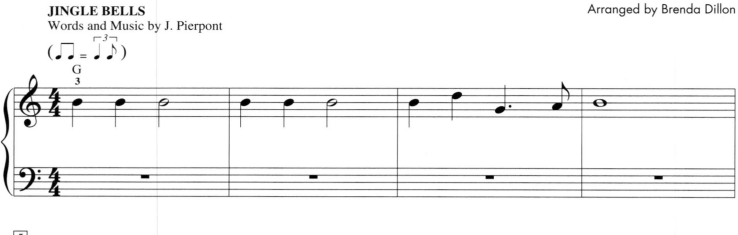

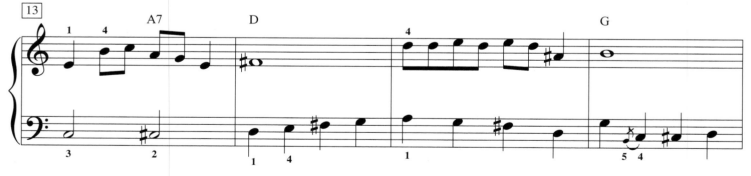

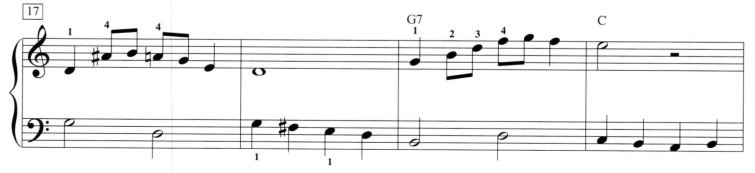

46

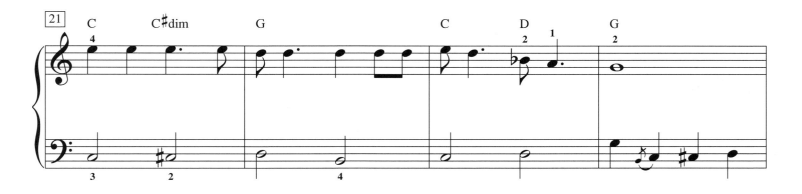

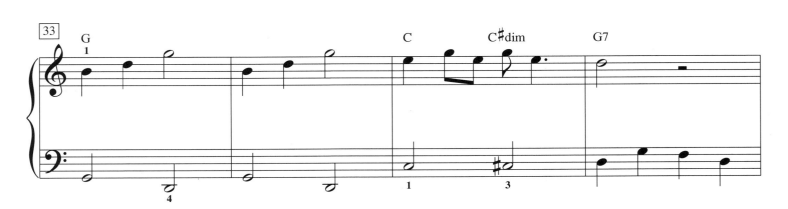

JOLLY OLD ST. NICHOLAS

Traditional 19th Century American Carol

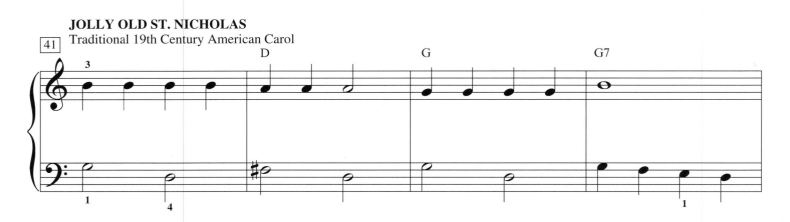

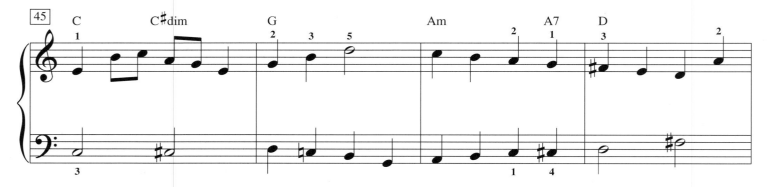

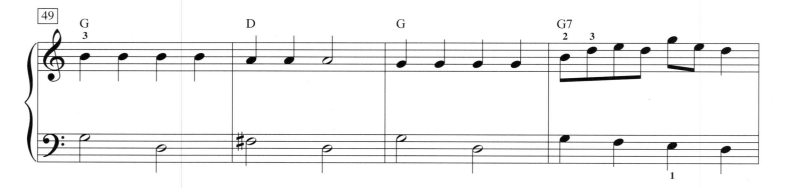

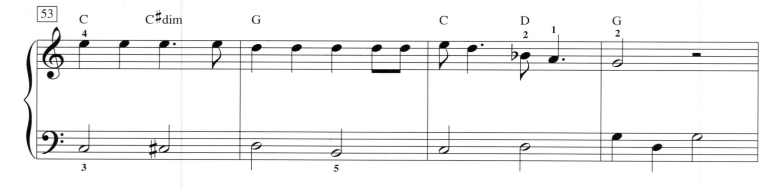

rit.

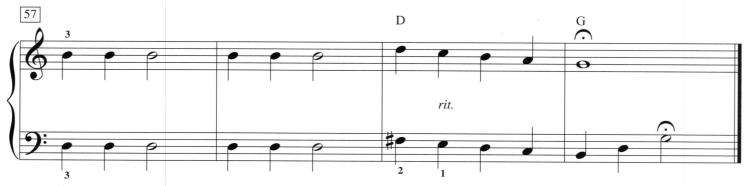